I0815360

An Imprint of Pop!
popbooksonline.com

The Eras of Taylor Swift

THE REPUTATION era

Track List

1. ...Ready For It?
2. End Game (ft. Ed Sheeran and Future)
3. I Did Something Bad
4. Don't Blame Me
5. Delicate
6. Look What You Made Me Do
7. So It Goes...
8. Gorgeous
9. Getaway Car
10. King of My Heart
11. Dancing with Our Hands Tied
12. Dress
13. This Is Why We Can't Have Nice Things
14. Call It What You Want
15. New Year's Day

by Grace Hansen

WELCOME TO DiscoverRoo!

This book is filled with videos, puzzles, games, and more! Scan the QR codes* while you read, or visit the website below to make this book pop.

popbooksonline.com/Rep

abdobooks.com
Published by Pop!, a division of ABDO, PO Box 398166, Minneapolis, Minnesota 55439.

Printed in the United States of America, North Mankato, Minnesota.

082025
012026

Cover Photo: Alexandra Tarasova (BigArtLab); Shutterstock Images
Interior Photos: Alamy; Getty Images; Shutterstock; PaoloV/Flickr; Everett Collection
Editors: Elizabeth Andrews and Anna Schwartz
Series Designer: Laura Graphenteen

Library of Congress Control Number: 2025941226

Publisher's Cataloging-in-Publication Data
Names: Hansen, Grace, author.
Title: The Reputation era / by Grace Hansen
Description: Minneapolis, Minnesota : Pop!, 2026 | Series: The eras of Taylor Swift | Includes online resources and index
Identifiers: ISBN 9781098248741 (lib. bdg.) | ISBN 9781098249267 (ebook)
Subjects: LCSH: Swift, Taylor, 1989- --Juvenile literature. | Popular music--Juvenile literature. | Popular (Songs, etc.)--Juvenile literature. | Albums--Juvenile literature. | Concerts--Juvenile literature. | Mass media and music--Juvenile literature.
Classification: DDC 782.42164099--dc23

*Scanning QR codes requires a web-enabled smart device with a QR code reader app and a camera.

TABLE OF CONTENTS

CHAPTER 1

BIG REPUTATION

On August 18, 2017, Taylor Swift fans and the media were buzzing. Taylor had blacked out her website and social media accounts. She removed everything that she had ever posted. People weren't sure what it meant. But they felt something big was coming.

WATCH A VIDEO HERE!

Meet Taylor

Birthday: December 13, 1989
Star Sign: Sagittarius
Place of Birth: West Reading, PA
Favorite Number: 13
Favorite Color: Purple
Favorite Meal: Chicken tenders and a chocolate shake

Benjamin Button

XOXO

Olivia Benson

Taylor Swift

On August 21, the first of three videos of a slithering snake hit Taylor's grid. On the 23rd, a post announced that the lead **single** for her sixth **studio** album would drop. The following day, "Look What You Made Me Do" was released. It quickly topped charts worldwide. Taylor was back. But she was different.

Taylor debuted a moody look for her **Reputation** *Era.*

A year prior, Taylor all but disappeared. The media had come after her time and time again. "They decided in 2016 that absolutely everything about me was wrong," Taylor remembered. People called her **calculating**, a fake, and a snake. They flooded her social media comments with snake emojis.

Taylor wore a lot of snake accessories during this era.

Taylor knew this time in her life was bound to happen. She couldn't always be on top. It was natural for people to want to pull her down. So, she withdrew from

Street artist Lushsux dedicated a giant mural to Taylor and encouraged people to leave flowers.

the public eye and surrounded herself with friends and family. When she was ready, she started writing again.

CHAPTER 2

READY FOR IT?

No one could have been ready for the *Reputation* album that dropped on November 10, 2017. Before then, fans had to survive off two **singles**: "Look What You Made Me Do" and "...Ready For It?" Both songs let people know exactly how Taylor felt when she wrote them. She was done playing nice. The old Taylor was dead.

EXPLORE LINKS HERE!

Critics and fans were impressed with Taylor's strong vocals in *Reputation*.

Easter Egg

In the "...Ready For It?" music video, Taylor references many things, including snakes. She cleverly placed "Year of the Snake" in Chinese characters on an alleyway sign.

THE SCANDAL THAT STARTED IT ALL

In 2016, artist Kanye West released the song "Famous." A line in the song mentions Taylor and calls her a swear word. Taylor spoke out against the line. Kanye and his then wife Kim Kardashian released an edited phone recording between the two parties where Taylor seemingly gave her approval. This turned the public against her. Later, in 2020, the full phone call came out, proving that Taylor was telling the truth.

Taylor said that writing *Reputation* was a "defense mechanism" for what she had gone through in 2016. She knew she had to shift her state of mind and take back her **narrative**. Instead of fighting against the snake allegations, Taylor completely **engulfed** herself in the persona.

The newspaper used for the Reputation *album art represents the negative narratives the media created about Taylor.*

Taylor brought together a small, trusted **production** team for *Reputation*. This would ensure a consistent album that was nothing like *1989*. Taylor executive produced *Reputation* and cowrote all 15 tracks. She wanted people to hear what she had to say.

Reputation ***set itself apart from Taylor's previous album*** **1989** ***in many ways.***

The sound of *Reputation* starts off strong and intense and ends on lighter notes. Taylor said this matched how she felt when she began writing the album and how she felt when it was finished. In its entirety, the album plays with darker tones, hip-hop, and **electropop**, but also has classic Swift sounds.

Much like the sound of the album, the themes are linear too. The start of the album centers more on revenge and drama, while the last half focuses on love and friendship. The album ends on the piano ballad "New Year's Day." The song brings up themes of new beginnings, finding peace, and cherishing lasting relationships.

DID YOU KNOW?

During Taylor's *Reputation* Era, her street style was often darker and edgier.

CHAPTER 3

BEHIND THE LYRICS

Reputation highlights Taylor's range both vocally and lyrically. "...Ready For It?" opens the album. Taylor felt this was the first song she wrote post-*1989* that was truly different. She also said imagery from the novel *Crime and Punishment*, such as "robbers, thieves, and heists," are found in the song and the rest of the album.

COMPLETE AN ACTIVITY HERE!

Crime and Punishment *was written by Russian author Fyodor Dostoyevsky.*

"Delicate" brings a softer sound to the album.

Sitting at number 5 on the track list and featuring soft vocals, "Delicate" is the album's most **vulnerable** song. Taylor said that the first few songs of *Reputation* are about not caring what people think of her. But, in "Delicate," the initial excitement of a new relationship leaves her worried that her reputation could affect her personal life.

"Look What You Made Me Do," track 6, began as a poem that Taylor had written. The song is about realizing that she could not let everyone into her life and that she had to cherish the few people she trusted. It's also about reinventing oneself and becoming wiser and stronger. Taylor said that the lyrics "I'm sorry, the old Taylor can't come to the phone right now. Why? Oh, 'cause she's dead" are the most important of the song.

Easter Egg

The "Look What You Made Me Do" music video features a throne covered in snakes and the phrase *Et tu, Brute?* (meaning "And you, Brutus?") carved into it. It references a line spoken by Julius Caesar, in William Shakespeare's play of the same name, when Julius realizes he has been betrayed by someone he trusted.

The second-to-last track on the album is "Call It What You Want." Taylor is the only writer credited on the song. The song **alludes** to Kanye West, Kim Kardashian, and others who had wronged her with the lyrics "All the liars are calling me one," "All the jokers dressing up as kings," and "All the drama queens taking swings." But Taylor knows that she did one thing right, which was choosing to date British actor

Taylor accepts the Top Female Artist award at the 2018 Billboard Music Awards.

Swift and Alwyn dated from 2016 to early 2023.

Joe Alwyn. Taylor and Joe began dating in late 2016, soon after Taylor's public reputation took a hit. The song lets people know that Joe stayed above the drama and loved her as if none of it had ever happened.

CHAPTER 4

ALL THE NICE THINGS

Ready to wow the public again, Taylor took *Reputation* on the road. The Reputation Stadium Tour kicked off on May 8, 2018, in Glendale, Arizona. Taylor played 53 shows across the United States and abroad.

LEARN MORE HERE!

More than 2.8 million people attended the Reputation Stadium Tour.

The Reputation Stadium Tour stage was dark and moody. The show opened with a video montage of Taylor and sounds clips of media gossip. Between each segment, imagery of a slithering snake appeared. The stage opened to reveal Taylor dressed in all black and thigh-high boots. She brought the mic up and asked, "Are you ready for it?"

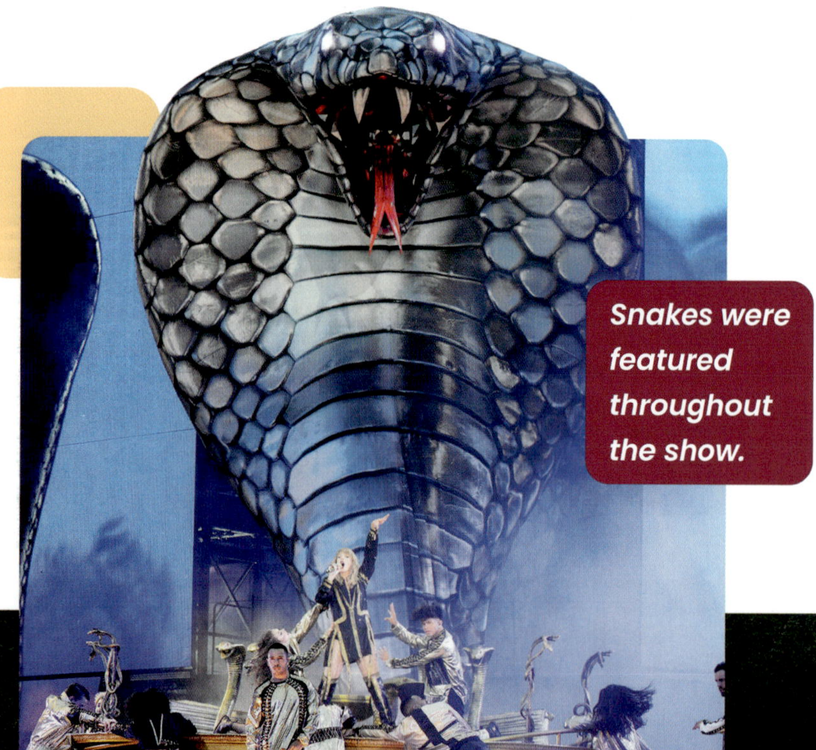

Snakes were featured throughout the show.

Taylor designed the Reputation Stadium Tour stage herself.

Taylor said the *Reputation* tour brought her back to a good place: "After that tour, bad stuff can happen to me, but it doesn't level me anymore."

Taylor performed "New Year's Day" from the piano.

Taylor also kicked off the *Reputation* set of the Eras Tour with "...Ready For It?" She devoted another three songs to the act with "Delicate," "Don't Blame Me," and "Look What You Made Me Do." The act was even more powerful because it was

DID YOU KNOW?

Reputation and "Blank Space" were both written from the perspective of who people thought Taylor was.

sandwiched between the *evermore* Era and the *Speak Now* Era, which have very different sounds and feels in comparison.

The *Reputation* Era featured the famous Roberto Cavalli one-legged catsuit. The costume was black and overlaid with red three-dimensional snakes. Taylor stuck with this version of the costume for most of her tour. But on October 18 in Miami, Florida, she **debuted** a fresh gold-and-black version. This got fans thinking that *Reputation (Taylor's Version)* was on its way.

A snake was wrapped around Taylor's microphone.

Taylor and her dancers brought the intensity in the Reputation *Era act.*

However, on May 30, 2025, in a heartfelt letter, Taylor let her fans know that she had purchased the rights back to her music catalog. She admitted that she had only rerecorded about a quarter of *Reputation*. She expressed that it was difficult for her to remake it:

"The *Reputation* album was so specific to that time in my life, and I kept hitting a stopping point.... To be perfectly honest, it's the one album in those first six that I thought couldn't be improved upon by redoing it."

MAKING CONNECTIONS

TEXT-TO-SELF

What is your favorite song from the *Reputation* Era? Why is it your favorite?

TEXT-TO-TEXT

Have you read books about any other music artists? How are they similar to or different from Taylor Swift?

TEXT-TO-WORLD

As a reader, why do you think so many people around the world connect with Taylor Swift and her music? Write a few sentences to explain your answer.

GLOSSARY

allude — to suggest or hint at.

calculating — planning and acting to accomplish a purpose.

debut — to appear for the first time.

electropop — a style of popular music that uses electronically created sounds, with a synthesizer as the primary instrument.

engulf — to surround completely.

narrative — a story, description, or account of events.

production — the act or process of producing. To produce is to organize the creation of music recordings.

single — a song that is released as a stand-alone from the album.

studio — a place where recordings are made.

vulnerable — open to being hurt emotionally.

INDEX

DiscoverRoo!
ONLINE RESOURCES

This book is filled with videos, puzzles, games, and more! Scan the QR codes* while you read, or visit the website below to make this book pop.

popbooksonline.com/Rep

*Scanning QR codes requires a web-enabled smart device with a QR code reader app and a camera.